SCIENCE-*OLOGY*

ZOOLOGY

ANNA CLAYBOURNE
DANIEL LIMÓN

PowerKiDS press

Published in 2026 by The Rosen Publishing Group, Inc.
2544 Clinton Street, Buffalo, NY 14224

First published in Great Britain in 2023 by Wayland

Editor: Elise Short
Consultant: Amy Cox, Learning Manager at The Royal Zoological Society of Scotland
Design: Rocket Design (East Anglia) Ltd
Illustrations: Daniel Limón

Cataloging-in-Publication Data
Names: Claybourne, Anna, author. | Limón, Daniel Sanchez, illustrator.
Title: Zoology / by Anna Claybourne, illustrated by Daniel Limón.
Description: Buffalo, NY : PowerKids Press, 2026. | Series: Science-ology | Includes glossary and index.
Identifiers: ISBN 9781499454819 (pbk.) | ISBN 9781499454826 (library bound) | ISBN 9781499454833 (ebook)
Subjects: LCSH: Zoology--Juvenile literature.
Classification: LCC QL49.C539 2026 | DDC 590--dc23

Picture credits: Alamy: Brandon Cole Marine Photography 10c; 35t Everett Collection Inc 35t; Imagebroker 5bl; Minden Pictures 5br, 43cl; pqpictures.co.uk 30c. Bimini Biological Field Station Foundation: 35b, 37t. Dreamtime: Tarpan 23cl. Getty Images: Galen Rowell 43t. Courtesy of Isle of Rum Red Deer Project: 34c. Nature PL: Tim Laman 25b. Shutterstock: Janis Abolins 27bcla; Aerial-motion 31t; Alfmaler 13br, 17bl; ALX1618 41tr; Andikaastro 11cl; Serafima Antipova 6c; Asharkyu 7c; Belander 23tr inset; Bismillah_Berkah 21c; Rich Carey 10t; Hung Chung Chih 4bl; Crbellette 15t; cusmin_35 20c; Djent 27bcr; Dos Gato Studio 17blc; Johnny Dream 12-13t; Fizkes 39c; Raphael Gaillarde 26bl; Dacian Galea 4c; GoodStudio 6br; Valeria Goryainova 16bl; GraphicRF 23tr inset; Andrey Gudkov 18c, 28t; Inspiring 26cl; Eric Isselee 31b; Jaddingt 33t; Ragne Kabanova 41t; Anita Kainrath 37c; Tory Kallman 23br; Kletr 17br; K3Star 25tr, 27cl; Lexamer 37br; Lolita Design 27bc; Love Media Lab 29cr; Luckyest 27bra; Macrovector 23tl, 26tl, 43c; Maquiladora 37cl, 37bl, 37bc; Martial Red 20cr; Masianya 13bl; Master3D 31cr; Metviser 27bl; NicoElNino 23bl; Noska Photo 38t; ODEBLAS 14tr; Guillermo Ossa 7tr; Paolo Pako 8b; Photoagriculture 4br; Photomatz 7tl; Olga Pogorelova 39tl; Pretty Vectors 39tr; Pyty 36t; Rapiraprap 23tr; Sakmeniko 27bca; Scottish Traveller 26br; Seahorse Vector 26clb; Fedor Selivanov 6bl; Se_vector 29cl; michael sheehan 35b; Shot Stalker 34t; SIM VA 20cl; Sirtravelalot 23c; Christopher Robin Smith Photography 32bl; Spreadthedesign 33c; Andrii Stepaniuk 13tr; Stock Unit 30t; STR110510 27bcra; Luke Suen 11b; Tasty_Cat 13cl; Paul Tessier 16br; The Leon King 27br; Vector Forever 27bla; Vectors Bang 42; Vektorkongen 13brc; Violart 18t;Kirsanov Valeriy Vladimirovich 29t; Voodoo Dot 27cl; Wavebreakmedia 25t; Richard Whitcombe 16tl; Lucy Y 26tr; Yganko 7bcl; Yiq 29b; Zentangle 26cr;Ru dmer Zwerver 40t.

Manufactured in the United States of America
CPSIA Compliance Information: Batch #CSPK26. For further information contact Rosen Publishing at 1-800-237-9932.

CONTENTS

UNDERSTANDING ANIMALS

Do you love animals and find them fascinating? Would you like to work with them and find out more about them? Then you'll love zoology, the science of animals.

What's it got to do with the zoo?

The word "zoology" sounds like it's about zoos. But it actually comes from two Greek words meaning "animal" and "study."

A zoo is called a zoo because it's short for "zoological gardens" – a place where scientists can study animals, and people can go to see them.

Some zoologists do work in zoos, studying animals or helping to make sure they have what they need. But they can be found in other places too ...

What zoologists do

All around the world right now, zoologists are busy ...

- **writing books and making TV shows about animals for people to enjoy;**

- **in schools and universities, studying animal science in the lab, and teaching zoology to students;**

WHY STUDY ZOOLOGY?

Science simply means "knowledge" – and humans study all kinds of things just because we want to know more about them. We're nosy like that!

But there are other important reasons to study zoology too.

- **Understanding animals so we can help keep them safe – or keep safe from them!**
- **Learning how animals help each other, and us too – for example, by pollinating our crops.**
- **Finding out how to save endangered animals from extinction.**
- **Observing how animals do things, which we can often learn from.**

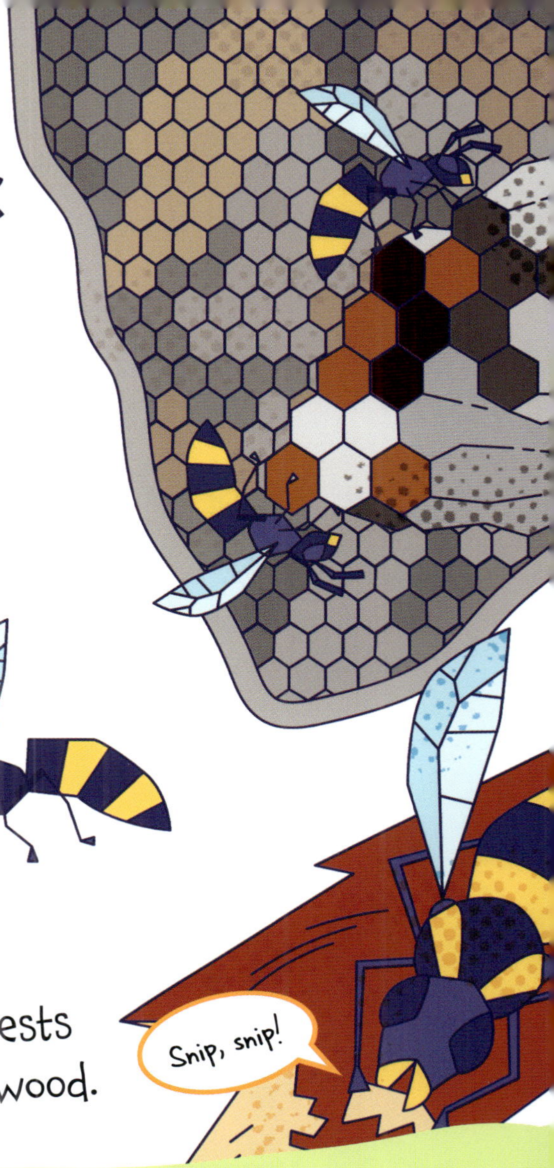

Watching wasps make their papery nests showed us how to make paper out of wood.

- **out in the wild, observing animals in their natural habitats – from icy mountains to steaming hot rainforests to underwater reefs;**
- **in wildlife reserves and field stations, such as the Bimini Shark Lab** **(see page 36).**

THE WORLD OF ZOOLOGY

There are a LOT of species, or types, of animals to learn about – over a million of them! So, zoology is divided up into different areas, or branches.

Which type of animal?

Some zoologists study a particular group or family of animals. For example, if you're really interested in reptiles, you could become a reptile scientist, or herpetologist. You could even focus on a single species, such as the large, fierce and very rare Komodo dragon.

Or what about ...

Cetology – the study of whales and dolphins

Felinology – the study of cats

Arachnology – the study of spiders

That's right – you could spend your whole life studying spiders, if that's what you're into!

ZOOLOGY THROUGH THE AGES

Since prehistoric times, humans have hunted and farmed animals, and kept them as pets. And for thousands of years we've also studied them and tried to learn more about them.

5000 years ago: Ancient Sumerians built early zoos.

2,300 years ago: Aristotle studied sea creatures, such as electric rays.

800s: Arabic scientist al-Jāḥiẓ wrote about hundreds of different animals.

Aspects of animals

There are other types of zoology too, such as ...

Anatomy

How animals' bodies work, and their shapes and body parts.

How do hummingbirds fly?

Evolution

The way species adapt and change over time.

Why were prehistoric sloths so much bigger than sloths today?

Animal behavior

How animals survive, communicate, learn, and interact.

How do ants tell each other where they've found food?

1100s: Hildegard of Bingen described fish and other animals in her science book *Physica*.

1700s: Carl Linnaeus came up with ways of sorting animals into groups and types.

1800s: Charles Darwin and Alfred Russel Wallace discovered how animal species evolve, or change, over time.

Today, there are more zoologists than ever!

WHICH IS WHICH?

How do you know that a bee is an insect, an owl is a bird, and lions are closely related to tigers? It's because zoologists sort animals, or classify them, into groups and types.

FINDING NEW SPECIES

One of the most exciting parts of zoology is finding a new species, previously unknown to science. Zoologists who discover a species have to investigate what type of animal it is, and where it belongs in the classification system.

Animal family tree

All living things are related, as they all evolved from the first simple living cells. Over time, new species developed, and split off from one another, like branches on a tree. So you can show the animal kingdom, and its main groups, as a big tree-shaped diagram. The branches show which species are closely related, and which are far apart.

Meet Chan's megastick!

Chan's megastick is a species of stick insect – one of the biggest in the world, with a body length of up to 14 inches (35 cm)!

What's in a name?

Zoologists give each animal species its own scientific name.

This means zoologists around the world always know which species they're talking about, even if they speak different languages. Here's an example:

The scientific name of Chan's megastick is

Phobaeticus chani

A scientific name has two parts, and usually describes the animal in some way.

"Phobaeticus" means "scary."

It's the name of a genus, or group, of extra-large stick insects.

- **Scientific names are always written in *italics*!**
- **The first part has a capital letter.**

"chani" comes from nature expert Datuk Chan Chew Lun, who reported the discovery of this stick insect in Malaysia in 1989.

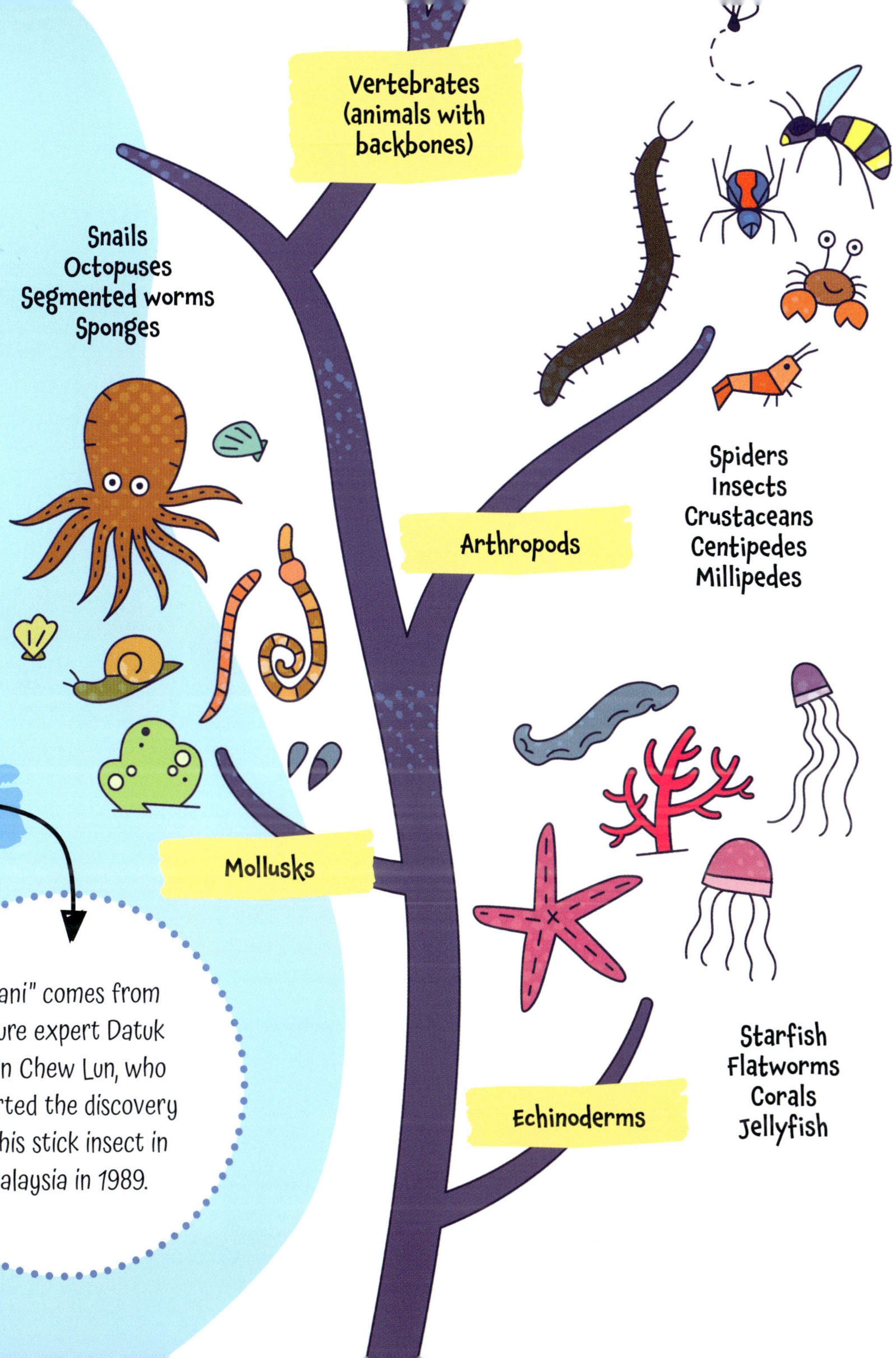

Case Study

Discovering an octopus

In 1998, three zoologists were diving off the coast of Indonesia when they spotted a strange octopus, unlike anything they had seen before.

Octopuses in disguise

The scientists were exploring and filming in shallow water when they saw the unusual octopus species on the sandy seabed. When in danger from predators, these octopuses changed position and color, imitating other, more dangerous sea creatures.

For example, an octopus could bury its body and six of its arms in the sand, leaving the other two out and wiggling them, so that they looked like a venomous sea snake.

Sea snake or octopus?

The octopuses could mimic other animals too:

ADVENTURE SKILLS!

Scientists who study octopuses and other sea creatures may have to go scuba diving to observe them in the wild. It's just one of several outdoor skills a zoologist might need:

More sightings

After a new species has been found, it may be spotted again in other places. Gradually zoologists build up a picture of its habitat, lifestyle, and where it can be found. We now know the mimic octopus lives in many different parts of the Pacific and Indian Oceans.

A new name

It usually takes a few years to study a newly discovered animal, to be sure it really is a separate species. Finally, in 2005, the octopus, known as the mimic octopus, was officially "described" as a new species and given a scientific name: *Thaumoctopus mimicus*. It means "Wondrous octopus mimic."

FACT FILE

MIMIC OCTOPUS

SCIENTIFIC NAME: *THAUMOCTOPUS MIMICUS*

SIZE: UP TO 24 INCHES (60 CM) ARMSPAN

HABITAT: SHALLOW, SANDY, OR MUDDY COASTAL SEABED

RANGE: INDIAN AND WESTERN PACIFIC OCEANS

DIET: SMALL FISH AND CRUSTACEANS

ANIMAL ANATOMY

Anatomy is about animal bodies. For example, how do birds' wings work, and how are birds light enough to fly? Zoologists are always asking questions like these and trying to find out the answers.

A closer look

You might have heard that birds have thin, light, hollow bones to make flying easier. But is that really true? How can light, thin wing bones be strong enough to flap without breaking? To find out, zoologists look at bird bones closely, including on the inside.

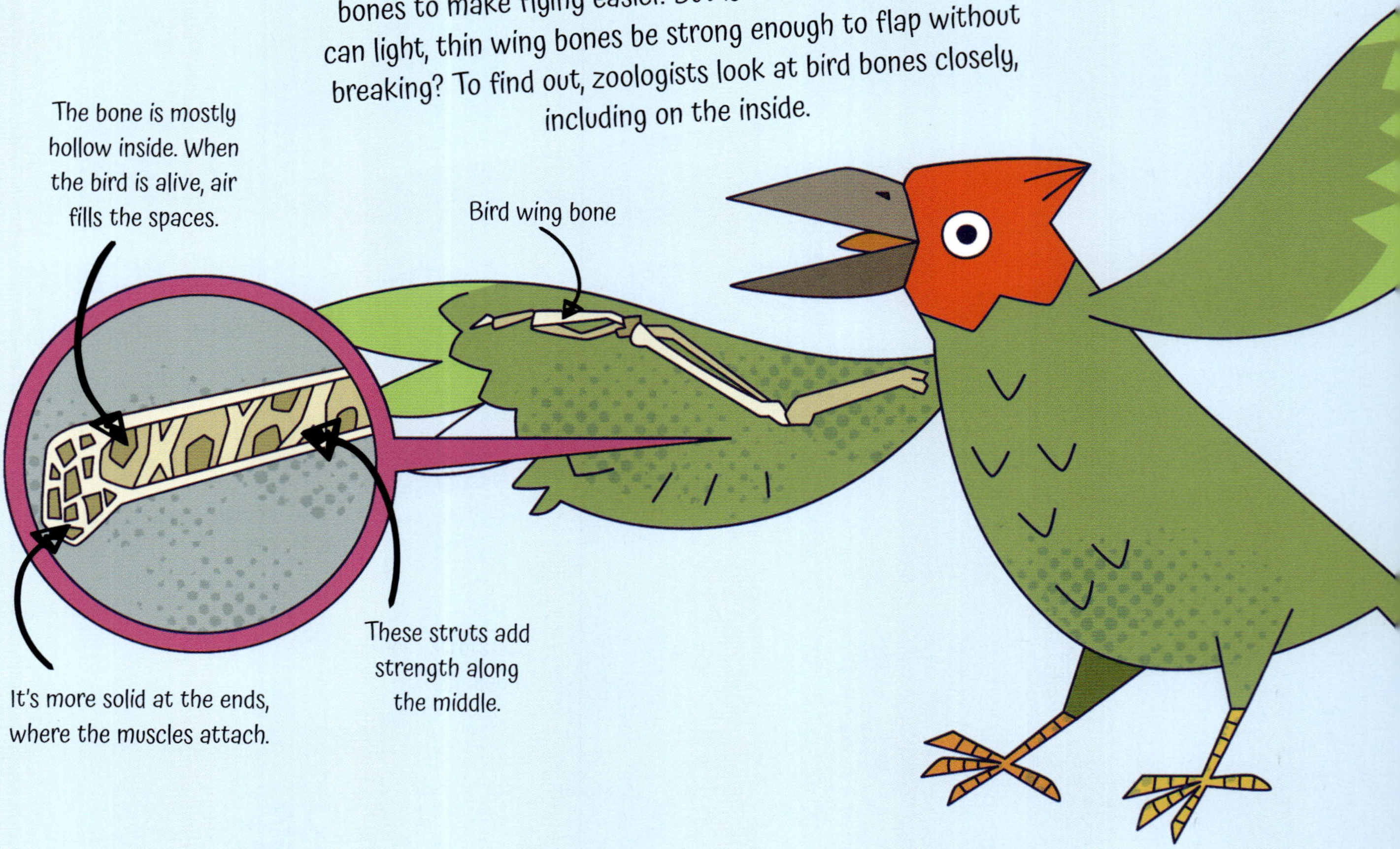

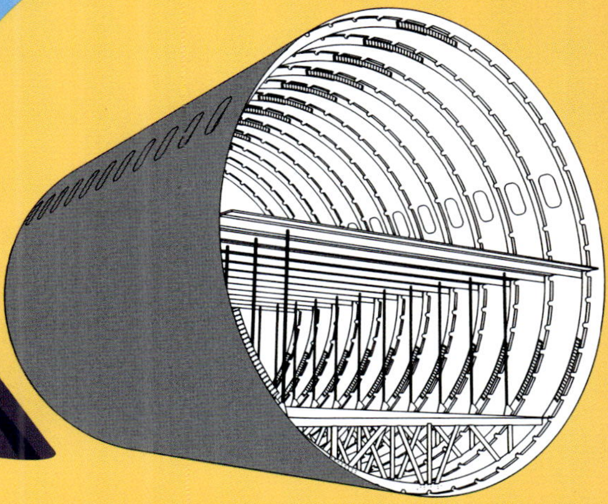

It's like building an aircraft out of metal. The metal is strong and heavy, but it's very thin, with air inside – so the plane is light for its size.

Super-strong bone

Zoologists have also measured the density of bird bone – how heavy it is for its size. To do this, they measure it carefully, using special equipment such as a helium pycnometer, which measures volume.

It turns out that bird bone itself is very strong and dense, or heavy for its size. It's actually heavier and denser than other types of animal bone! This makes bird bones extra-strong. But the bone as a whole is quite light, because of its long thin shape and the space inside it.

Zoology departments and museums have collections of animal bones and skeletons for scientists to use – so they don't have to go and catch animals to study all the time!

WHAT DOES THIS DO?

Some animals have really unusual body parts. Zoologists are still debating what these are for ...

- The male narwhal's tusk, formed from an extra-long front tooth

- The cassowary's hard, hollow crest or "casque"

- The unique helicopter shape on this treehopper insect's head!

ANIMAL BEHAVIOR

As an animal behavior zoologist, you watch animals living their lives – doing things like hunting, building a home, caring for their babies, or looking for a mate. It's fascinating, but not always easy!

Watching animals

One problem is that many animals don't like being watched. If birds realize people are nearby, they might fly away. A fierce animal like a tiger could even attack you. And just by being there, zoologists can make animals behave differently from normal. So zoologists often use observation hides (or blinds), powerful binoculars and telescopic cameras to watch animals from a distance.

A bird blind lets you watch birds without them seeing you. This is a floating blind for studying water birds.

In captivity

It's sometimes easier to observe animal behavior in captive animals, in a lab or zoo. Tiny peacock spiders are found in Australia. To study their courtship displays, zoologists collect the spiders from the wild and keep them in the lab. They give them soil, leaves, and twigs from their natural habitat, their favorite insects to eat, and natural lighting.

To watch the spiders displaying, they are put in a special study area.

A male peacock spider attracts a female by lifting up his colorful abdomen.

Zoologists have to use microscopes and special cameras to see the displays clearly, because peacock spiders are so small – only 0.2 inch (5 mm) long!

New ideas

Sometimes, animals come up with new ideas or inventions, and copy them from each other. In one famous case, zoologists went to study macaques (a type of monkey) on Koshima Island in Japan. One day, a monkey known as Imo washed a potato in a stream to get the sand off. The others copied her, and the behavior spread all over the island.

WHAT ANIMALS DO

There's a huge range of animal behavior to study, such as ...

- Mating dances
- Hunting methods
- Storing food
- Fighting
- Home building
- Working as a team
- Teaching young
- Playing
- Migrating

Can you think of any more?

HOW ANIMALS TALK

We can't talk to animals in the same way we chat, tell stories, or explain things to each other. But that doesn't mean animals can't talk!

Sending signals

Animals send each other signals and messages all the time using a variety of methods and senses.

Squid and cuttlefish flash patterns and colors across their skin to signal to a mate, or warn off an enemy. This pattern means: "I'm looking for a mate."

Ants, wolves, and many other animals use smell to communicate. Deer are amazing at this! They release scent chemicals from their bodies to tell other deer their age, whether they're male or female, and where their territories are, and to warn each other of danger.

What's that I smell?

Lots of species call to each other, and some have different calls for saying different things. Blackbirds make a "Seeee!" warning call when they spot a hunting bird in the air, but call "Pook-pook" when there's a hunter on the ground, such as a cat.

Listening in

Humpback whales make clicking, squeaking, and moaning sounds to talk to each other, and sing long, complex songs to attract a mate.

To hear them, zoologists lower a device called a hydrophone under the water to collect and record the sounds.

Animals are not humans!

Zoologists have to remember not to "anthropomorphize" animals, or assume they are like humans. When a chimpanzee makes this face, for example, it might look to us like laughing – but chimps actually do this when they're upset or scared.

SPEAKING OUR LANGUAGE

A few animal species can learn to understand human words. Dogs, for example, learn what words like "walk" mean. One dog, a collie named Rico, learned over 200 words!

Others, especially some birds, can learn to say human words too.

HOW SMART ARE ANIMALS?

How can we test animals' intelligence, when we can't ask them questions or make them sit for an exam? This is a big challenge for zoologists.

What is intelligence?

This is a hard question to answer, even in humans. There are many different ways of being smart. However, most scientists agree that intelligence includes things such as:

- **Learning fast**
- **Understanding how things work**
- **Planning ahead**
- **Adapting to different situations**
- **Inventing new ways to do things.**

To measure intelligence, zoologists have to come up with tests and experiments that animals can do.

In this test, a Caledonian crow shows it can plan ahead to solve a problem.

1 A snack is floating in a jar out of reach.

2 By adding stones, the crow makes the water level rise.

3 Then it can grab the snack!

Intelligence or instinct?

Intelligence is not the same thing as instinct. An instinct is something an animal does automatically and doesn't have to learn.

This spider can spin a beautiful, intricate web – but web spinning is an instinct, not a sign of learning skills or being inventive.

The smartest species

You might think the smartest animals would be close relatives of humans, such as chimps. Apes and monkeys do show high intelligence, but so do several other animals, such as:

- **Ants**
- **Rats**
- **Birds (especially crows and parrots)**
- **Pigs**
- **Elephants.**

Rats can remember routes from previous journeys and so are able to navigate their way out of a maze.

Is that me?

When you look in a mirror, you know that you're seeing a reflection of yourself. But can animals figure it out?

To do a mirror test, zoologists put a mark on an animal's face while it's asleep. It can't feel the mark. Later, they show it a mirror. If it tries to touch or rub off the mark on its own face, that means it realizes that it is seeing itself.

Only a few species have passed the test. They include chimpanzees, orangutans, bottlenose dolphins, orcas, magpies, some elephants, and amazingly, ants!

Aren't we clever!

Case Study

Alex the parrot

Most people know that parrots can copy human words. But a parrot named Alex showed that they can do much more!

Working with Alex

Alex was an African grey, a large parrot native to Africa, and sometimes kept as a pet. In 1977, animal scientist Irene Pepperberg bought Alex, who was about one year old, from a pet shop in Chicago, Illinois. She wanted to study the way parrots use words, and whether they simply copy them, or can also understand their meaning.

FACT FILE

AFRICAN GREY PARROT

LATIN NAME: ***PSITTACUS ERITHACUS***

SIZE: 14 INCHES (35 CM) LONG

HABITAT: RAINFORESTS

RANGE: CENTRAL AFRICA

DIET: SEEDS, NUTS, BERRIES, AND FRUIT

Learning words

To train Alex, Pepperberg let him watch her talking to an assistant about words and objects. Alex began to join in and copy them, learning different words for different things. Eventually, he learned over 100 words, and could name different objects.

Alex's amazing abilities

As time went on, Alex learned other things too. He knew color and shape words and what they meant. He could express his feelings, and would say "no" or "wanna go back" if he didn't feel like doing a test. He could even count, as this experiment showed.

- **Pepperberg showed Alex a tray of blocks in three colors.**
- **She would ask a question such as, "What color five?"**
- **Alex could tell her which color there were five of.**

Bird brains

Pepperberg's work revealed that birds can be very intelligent. Previously, most scientists thought only mammals, such as chimps and dolphins, could be this smart.

Alex said these words to Pepperberg each night:

Sadly, Alex died unexpectedly in 2007 at age 31 (African greys usually live longer than this). But zoologists around the world are still studying bird intelligence.

HABITATS AND ECOSYSTEMS

An animal's habitat is the place it lives in, such as a coral reef, a garden, or a desert. Ecology is the science of habitats and the living things in them. A habitat, along with the living things in it, is known as an ecosystem.

Living together

In any habitat, there's a variety of animals and other living things, like plants, fungi, and bacteria. They feed on each other and depend on each other to survive. Zoologists show this as a diagram called a food web.

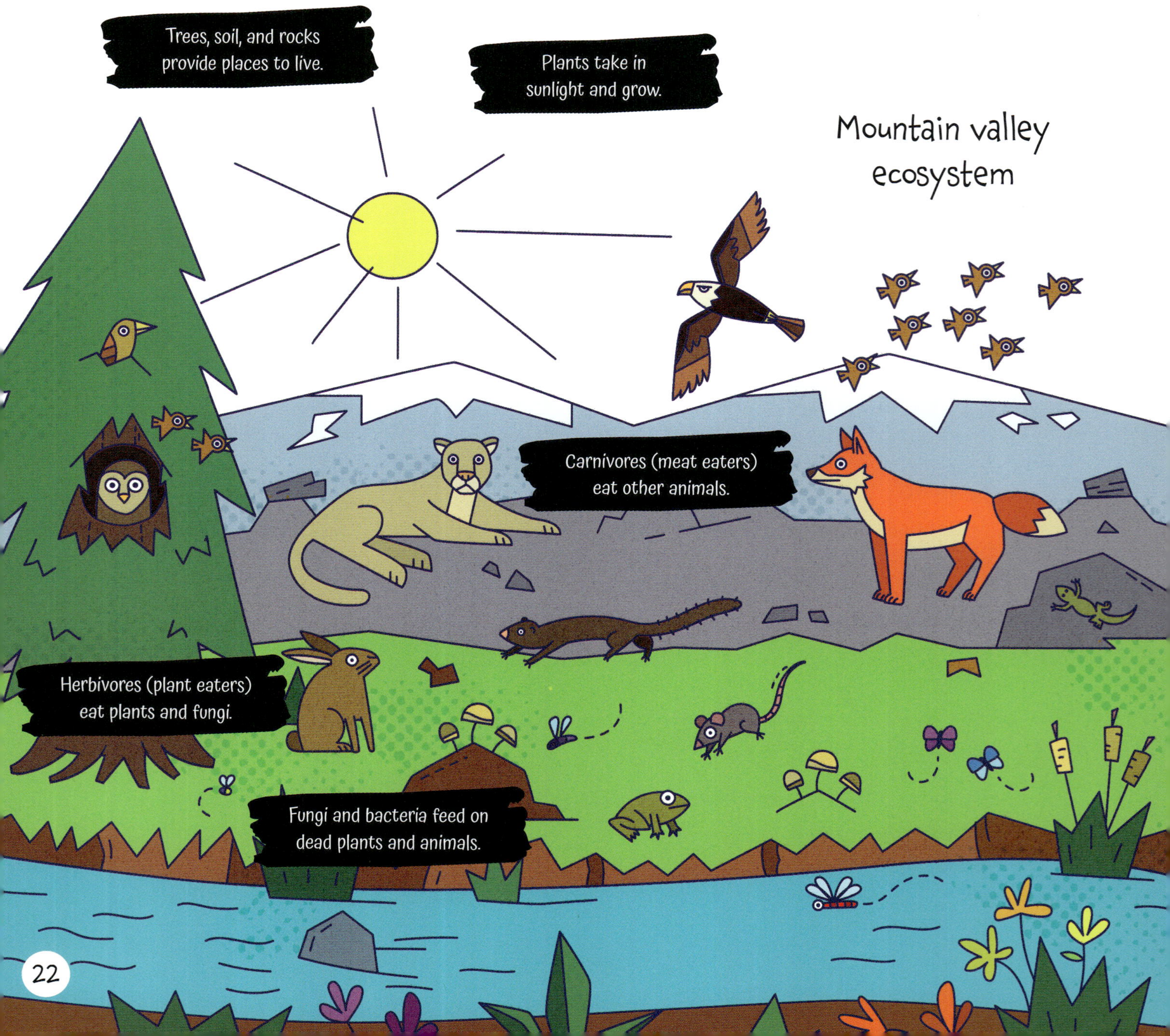

Studying ecology

Studying ecosystems helps zoologists learn about animals in their environment. But as you can imagine, it's tricky keeping track of a whole group of living things. To do it, zoologists use three main methods:

- **Observation**

Watching, listening, counting, taking photos, making notes.

- **Experiments**

Making a change to see what happens.

- **Modeling**

Making a computer simulation of an ecosystem, so they can experiment with that too.

Understanding changes

Things like pollution, flooding, or climate change can change an ecosystem. Zoologists study how this affects the living things in it.

For example, in the Antarctic, numbers of Adélie penguins are falling – but why?

1. Adélies often eat small crustaceans called krill.

2. Krill feed on algae that grow under ice.

3. Global warming is melting ice, so there's less algae.

That could mean fewer krill and less food for Adélie penguins.

4. Fewer Adélies could be a problem for animals that eat them, such as orcas.

ENDANGERED SPECIES

Thousands of animal species are endangered, or at risk of dying out and becoming extinct. Zoologists can help!

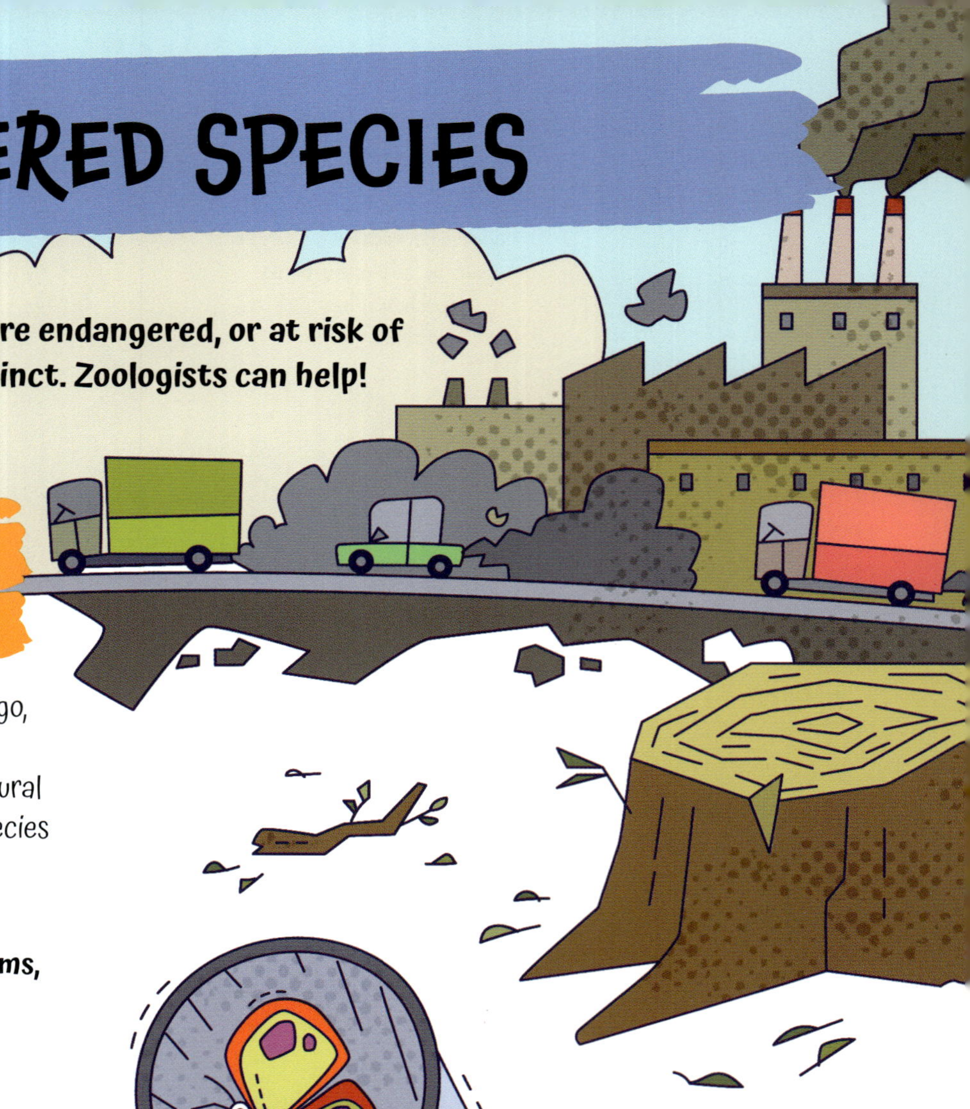

Why do animals become extinct?

Since life began almost 4 billion years ago, millions of species – the dinosaurs, for example – have died out because of natural events. Now, though, more and more species are dying out due to human activities. Activities that harm wildlife include:

- **Taking over wild habitats for our farms, towns, and roads**
- **Hunting and collecting wild animals**
- **Polluting the land, air, and water**
- **Causing global warming, which changes animal habitats.**

Is it endangered?

To find out which species are endangered, zoologists monitor wild species, counting them to see if they are becoming less common. This is especially important when a natural habitat, such as a rainforest, is disappearing.

Sometimes, a species is already endangered when zoologists first discover it – as with the Cape Melville leaf-tailed gecko, discovered in an Australian mountain rainforest in 2013. It's at risk because:

- **it only has a small area of forest habitat**
- **global warming is making the forest hotter and drier, which the geckos don't like**
- **people collect them to sell as exotic pets.**

This zoologist is teaching children about wild animal conservation.

WHAT CAN WE DO?

There are several systems in place to help endangered species, and zoologists often help to run them or set them up.

- **Wildlife reserves to keep natural habitats safe**
- **Laws against hunting and collecting endangered animals**
- **Keeping endangered species in zoos and helping them to breed**
- **Helping people learn about endangered species and how to protect them.**

ENDANGERED RATINGS

Zoologists around the world work with the International Union for Conservation of Nature, or IUCN, to give each animal a conservation status - a rating that shows how endangered it is.

LC	Least Concern (not at risk)
NT	Near Threatened
VU	Vulnerable
EN	Endangered
CR	Critically Endangered
EW	Extinct in the Wild
E	Extinct

The Cape Melville leaf-tailed gecko is listed as EN.

The endangered Cape Melville leaf-tailed gecko

IN THE FIELD

Most zoologists spend some time "in the field" – that is, in the wild. They visit natural habitats to observe and monitor the animals there.

Wild world

Animals live in all kinds of wild, remote, hard-to-reach or even dangerous places. Working in the field could mean ...

- **Exploring thick rainforests, sometimes at night**
- **Being out at sea in a boat, or deep underwater in a mini-submarine**
- **Climbing up high trees or cliffs, or down into spooky caves**
- **Freezing on an icy mountaintop or Antarctic glacier**
- **Trekking across a sweltering desert.**

Imagine working here! An inflatable "canopy raft" is lowered onto rainforest trees by an airship or helicopter. Zoologists can move around on it to study animals that live in the rainforest canopy, or upper level.

Or how about landing a boat at Ball's Pyramid off the coast of Australia, then climbing up it to search for the rare Lord Howe Island stick insect?

It was thought to be extinct, until it was found living on this steep rocky pinnacle.

Local experts

Zoologists may know a lot about animal science, but local people often know more about where a particular animal lives, or the safest paths through a forest or swamp. So zoologists often work with a local guide who knows the area and can help them find the species they're looking for.

When zoologists go to monitor tiny, rare Sokoke scops owls in Kenya, a local guide shows them the way through the forest, and makes owl calls, which the real owls answer.

DON'T FORGET YOUR GEAR!

Zoologists have to lug all kinds of equipment on field trips too!

- GPS and maps
- Safety gear
- Flashlight
- Binoculars
- First aid kit
- Sound recording equipment
- Camera or video camera
- Sun protection
- Water and snacks
- Insect repellent

Case Study

Tiger tracking

Amur tigers are very rare, good at hiding, and extremely dangerous! So how do zoologists keep track of where they are?

The amazing Amur

The Amur or Siberian tiger, the biggest of all tigers, lives in cold northern forests in China and Russia. Due to hunting and logging, it almost died out in the 1940s, when there were only around 30 Amur tigers left.

Today, anti-hunting laws and wildlife reserves have increased this number to over 300 wild Amur tigers, but they're still endangered. Tracking their movements is important to make sure wildlife reserves are put in the right places and to monitor how many Amur tigers there are.

FACT FILE

AMUR TIGER

SCIENTIFIC NAME: *PANTHERA TIGRIS ALTAICA*

SIZE: 8-10 FEET (2.5–3 M) LONG, INCLUDING THE TAIL

HABITAT: COLD NORTHERN FORESTS

RANGE: PARTS OF EASTERN RUSSIA AND NORTHEAST CHINA

DIET: DEER, WILD BOAR, AND SMALLER ANIMALS

Tracking methods

Zoologists track these tigers in several ways.

• On the ground

They follow the trails tigers leave on the snowy ground, and look out for other signs such as droppings and scratch marks.

A zoologist checks Amur tiger droppings.

• Collar tracking

For this method, zoologists have to find tigers and use darts to put them to sleep, then fit them with a tracking collar. The collar sends out signals that are picked up by radio receivers or GPS satellites, and made into maps showing the tigers' movements.

• Camera traps

A camera trap is an automatic camera that takes a photo when something moves in front of it. Zoologists have set up hundreds of camera traps where Amur tigers live and use the photos of tigers to make maps showing where they are.

Types of tigers

All tigers are the same species, but there are different types, or subspecies, in different places. For example, the Bengal tiger is found mainly in India and the smaller Sumatran tiger in Indonesia.

Sumatran tiger

Bengal tiger

Amur tiger

IN THE LAB

Though a lot of zoology happens in the field, some zoologists spend more time in the science lab. Get your white coat on!

This zoologist is working with animal skeletons in a lab.

Under the microscope

Using microscopes, zoologists can take a close look at animal cells and body parts to see how they work.

For example, squid, cuttlefish (see page 16), and octopuses (see pages 10–11) can change color in a flash, using patterns on their skin to send messages. But how do they do that?

A microscope shows that their skin contains special color-making cells called chromatophores.

Each chromatophore can quickly shrink or expand, changing how much of each color appears on the skin.

Expanding

Shrinking

Experiments

Zoologists also do experiments in the lab, sometimes using living animals. For example, seawater is becoming more acidic because of extra carbon dioxide in the atmosphere. To see how this affects the shells of sea creatures, zoologists keep animals such as clams or sea snails in the lab, and see what happens to their shells in slightly more or less acidic water.

Animals such as sea snails are affected by acid levels in the sea.

Experiments like these have shown that higher acidity can weaken and damage seashells and coral.

Animal genes

Zoologists also study animals' genes, made up of DNA. They are instructions inside cells that control how living things look and how their bodies work.

This can reveal how animals are related. For example, genetic studies showed that chickens and turkeys are the closest living relatives of dinosaurs.

The axolotl is an amazing amphibian that can regrow its limbs if it loses them. Zoologists are studying its genes to try to find out how this works.

SCIENCE METHODS

When you do experiments, such as the ocean acidity experiment above, you have to make sure they are carefully set up and reliable.

For example, you should keep all your sea creatures in the exact same conditions, apart from the water acidity. That way, if there's a difference, you know that's what caused it.

ANIMAL DISEASES

Just like humans, animals can get a wide range of illnesses. Some are mild, but others can be deadly, and a few can spread to humans too.

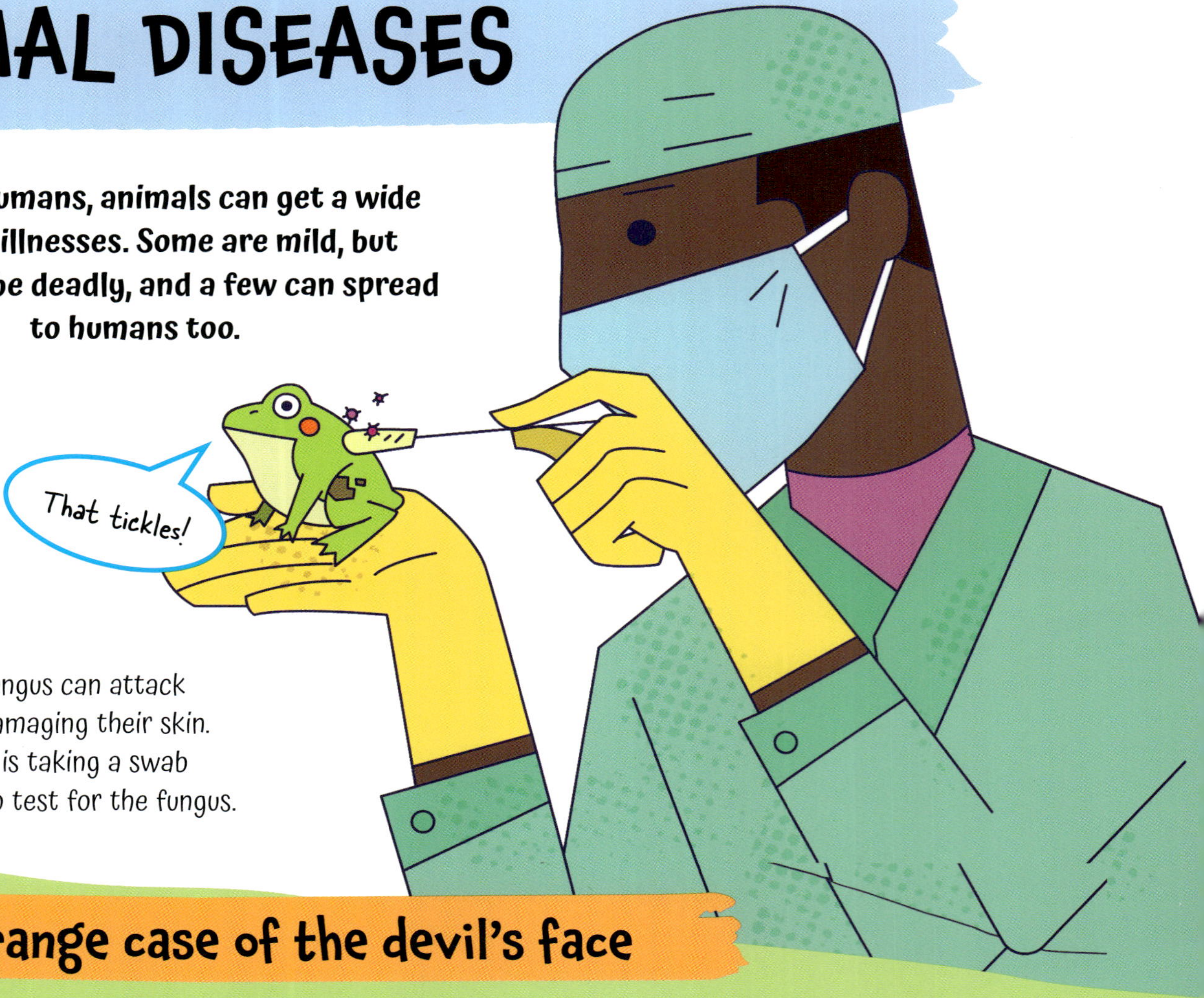

The chytrid fungus can attack amphibians, damaging their skin. This zoologist is taking a swab from a frog to test for the fungus.

The strange case of the devil's face

The Tasmanian devil is an unusual mammal from the island of Tasmania in Australia. It looks a bit like a giant rat with an extra-large head, but it's actually a marsupial, related to kangaroos and koalas.

A healthy Tasmanian devil

In the 1990s, farmers noticed that some Tasmanian devils had a disease on their faces, and often died from it. Zoologists took samples from the diseased devils, and studied the cells and DNA. They found the disease was a type of cancer.

Animal vaccines

Ebola is another disease that can affect animals. In parts of Africa, this deadly virus has killed thousands of chimps and gorillas – especially bad news as they're already endangered.

After studying the disease in apes, scientists developed a vaccine, which has worked well on chimps and gorillas in tests.

Zoologists often work with vets, zookeepers, and other scientists and experts to find the best way to tackle animal diseases.

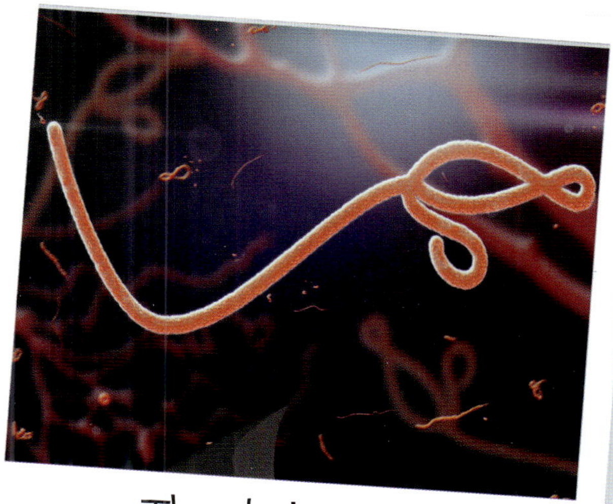

The Ebola virus

A bite from a bat could give you rabies, another deadly disease.

TAKE CARE!

Ebola and some other animal diseases can also affect humans. Zoologists have to be extremely careful when they work with sick animals and wear protective gear, such as gloves and masks.

They also watched Tasmanian devils in the field. They found that the disease seemed to spread between devils when they fought and bit each other's faces.

They monitored the devils to keep track of the disease. To try to stop it from wiping the species out, they moved several groups of disease-free devils to other areas.

LONG-TERM STUDIES

Zoologists often work in the field for a few days or weeks. But some spend years there, making long-term studies of animals such as orcas, elephants, apes, or insects.

Cicadas emerging as adults after spending years underground

Changing over time

A long-term study can reveal interesting things that you can't tell by just watching animals for a short time. For example ...

• 17-year cicadas

In the eastern United States, long-term studies have shown how periodical cicadas have a superlong life cycle, of either 13 or 17 years.

When they hatch out of their eggs, cicada nymphs (babies) spend either 13 or 17 years feeding underground. Then millions of adults all emerge at the same time to find a mate. This helps the species survive, as there are too many for predators to eat.

• Red deer island

On the Isle of Mull in Scotland, zoologists have been studying red deer for 70 years! Dozens of zoologists have taken part. One scientist stays on the island all year round to monitor the deer, while others come on field trips.

The chimps of Gombe

In 1960, British primatologist Jane Goodall went to find out more about chimpanzees in the rainforests of Tanzania – and this study is still going today. Goodall lived in the Gombe Stream National Park with the chimps for over 20 years, making some important discoveries:

- **Chimps were not vegetarians, as people had thought.**
- **They could use tools, such as poking a stick into a termite mound to catch termites. Before this, scientists thought that only humans used tools.**
- **They were not always peaceful – they sometimes had violent fights, and even wars between groups.**

Jane Goodall observing a chimpanzee family

ANIMAL NICKNAMES

Zoologists often give each animal in their study a nickname to help tell them apart – such as Sycamore, Canuck 2, or David Greybeard.

What names would you give this family of elephants?

Case Study

Bimini Shark Lab

Imagine living in the Bahamas, and waking up to go swimming with baby sharks in a beautiful lagoon. That's life for the staff and volunteers at the Bimini Shark Lab. (Well, some of the time!)

Shark studies

There are countless movies and books about sharks, but we actually don't know that much about their lives. They are hard to keep in captivity, and hard to follow as they zoom around the oceans.

So in 1990, American shark expert Dr. Samuel Gruber set up a new base on South Bimini island in the Bahamas, where zoologists could study sharks in the wild. Its official name is the Bimini Biological Field Station, but it's known worldwide as Bimini Shark Lab.

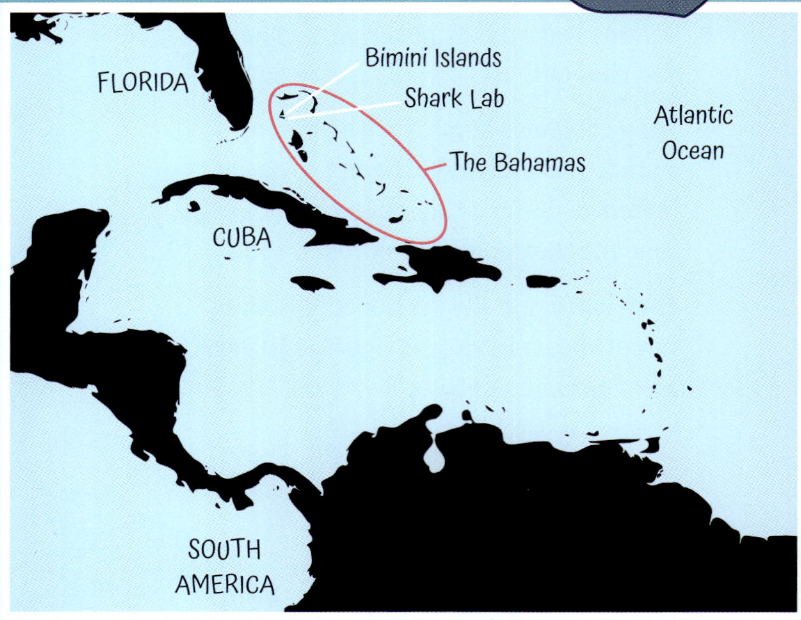

The lab is a wooden building with bedrooms and a kitchen, a science lab room, and its own dock with a fleet of boats.

FACT FILE

LEMON SHARK

LATIN NAME: *NEGAPRION BREVIROSTRIS*

SIZE: UP TO 11 FEET (3.4 M) LONG

HABITAT: WARM, USUALLY SHALLOW SEAS NEAR THE COAST

RANGE: ATLANTIC AND EASTERN PACIFIC OCEANS

DIET: FISH, CRUSTACEANS, AND SHELLFISH

Working with sharks

At Bimini, zoologists and students study sharks and other sea life, especially lemon sharks. These yellowish-brown, shallow-water sharks are common in the area, and are known for being gentle and friendly. Everyday tasks include:

- **Photographing, measuring, and weighing sharks**
- **Tagging and tracking sharks to monitor their movements**
- **Writing up results**
- **Training volunteers**
- **Taking visiting tourists to see the sharks**
- **Looking after the station, fixing equipment, cleaning, and cooking.**

A zoologist scans a baby lemon shark fitted with an ID chip, like the ones we use in pet cats and dogs.

Studies at the lab show that young lemon sharks live in "shark nurseries," sheltering among mangrove tree roots near the shore. As they grow up, they leave, but females later return to have their own babies.

More sharks!

The shark lab also studies other sharks and their relatives – rays.

ANIMALS AND US

Animals are an important part of life for most humans. Some zoologists, known as anthrozoologists, study our relationships with them.

We train some animals to work for us, like these earthquake rescue dogs.

Animal world

Our relationships with animals can be positive or negative – or both.

We love our pets ...

... enjoy watching wildlife ...

... and try to help endangered species.

But we also damage animal habitats ...

... kill species that we see as pests ...

... and farm and eat animals.

Farming

We farm animals for meat, milk, eggs, wool, and other things. Some people don't think we should do this at all – vegans, for example, try not to use any kind of animal product.

But animal farming is still a huge industry around the world. By understanding farm animals and their experiences, zoologists can help to improve their lives.

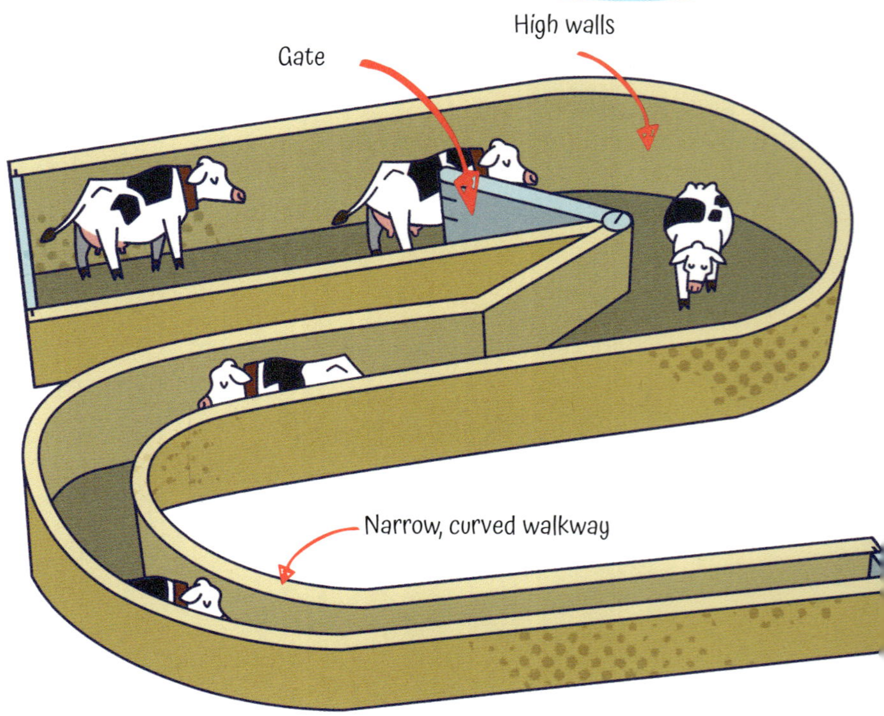

Animal expert Temple Grandin has invented new systems for moving farm animals around, using curved, narrow walkways that help them to stay calm.

Humans and dogs

Pet dogs don't exist in the wild. Humans "domesticated" them long ago from a wild wolf species, using selective breeding – choosing only animals with useful qualities for breeding, so that the species changes over time. Most farm animals are domesticated too.

All dog breeds are the same species, descended from wild wolves.

Humans often feel a very close bond with dogs.

Some zoologists study domestication and how it works. They think dogs and humans, for example, have evolved together to understand each other's facial expressions.

HOW WE FEEL ABOUT ANIMALS

We often feel strongly about animals.

For example, you might love cats, but find slugs horrifying. This is important in conservation, because people are more likely to want to help cute or lovable endangered species.

Zoologists study this too, and sometimes use social media campaigns to help make "ugly" endangered species more popular.

Who wants to save the endangered purple frog?

ANIMAL INSPIRATION

How can geckos walk on the ceiling? How do termite mounds keep cool? We can use this kind of zoological knowledge in human designs and inventions, in the high-tech science of bionics.

Amazing adaptations

Over time, living things evolve to suit their surroundings, or adapt. This gives them all kinds of useful features and abilities, which zoologists study to see how they work.

Geckos have millions of tiny hair-like "setae" on their feet, giving them a larger area of contact with what they are walking on. The setae grip the surface so strongly that the gecko can stick to a ceiling.

Inspiration

Idea

A kind of sticky tape that works like gecko feet, and a gecko robot that can climb walls.

When the Namib desert beetle lifts its body into the foggy air, water droplets collect on water-attracting bumps on its back, and flow down into its mouth.

Inspiration

Idea

Water-collecting devices that use the same method as the desert beetle.

That's a good idea!

In bionics labs, zoologists work with engineers and designers to make animal-inspired inventions.

Here, Spot!

Spot is a famous dog-inspired robot that can run, carry things, and get up if it falls over.

It could be used as a rescue dog so that real dogs are not put in danger.

An elephant's trunk has no bones, but uses many powerful muscles to move in any direction.

Inspiration

Idea

A multi-directional robot limb, based on the elephant's trunk.

Termites build their mounds with tall chimneys. As hot air rises up them, it sucks fresh, cooler air through the termites' tunnels.

Inspiration

Idea

Self-cooling buildings in Zimbabwe, inspired by termite mounds.

A shark's skin is covered with tiny tooth-like "denticles", which help it slip more easily through the water, and also kill bacteria.

Inspiration

Idea

A sharkskin-inspired surface that kills germs, and can be used to coat toilet flush handles and other surfaces where germs could collect.

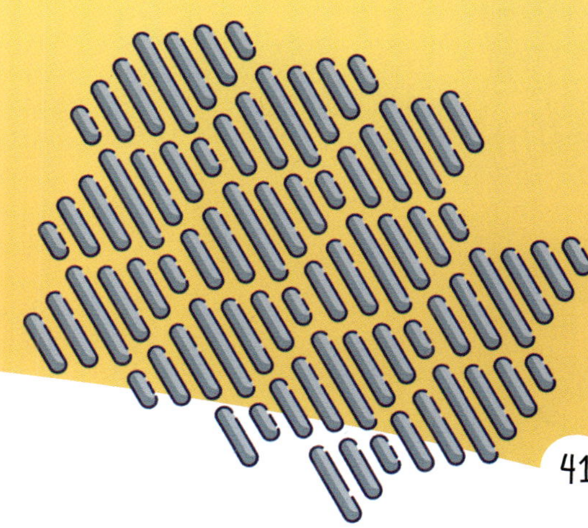

ETHICS

"Ethics" means rights and wrongs. Zoologists have to follow ethical guidelines to make sure they treat animals with respect and try not to harm or upset them.

Changing attitudes

In the past, many people – including scientists – didn't care as much about animals as we do today. It was normal to do all kinds of experiments on animals, and to take birds' eggs and insects from the wild to keep in collections.

A collection of birds' eggs from the 1800s.

Even the famous zoologist Charles Darwin collected eggs and insects.

THE DOG WITH TWO HEADS

Shockingly, in 1959, a scientist named Vladimir Demikhov transplanted a dog's head onto the back of another living dog. This would be considered totally unethical today and would not be allowed.

ANIMAL CARE RULES

Today, most countries have laws to protect animals, and zoologists use ethical guidelines for treating the animals they're working with as well as possible.

- **Always treat animals gently and respectfully.**
- **Only experiment on live animals if there's a good reason, and use as few as possible.**
- **Lab animals must be well-cared for, given suitable homes and food, and be free from pain and suffering.**
- **Don't use a live animal for an experiment if you could use a preserved animal or animal part, such as a bone, from an existing collection.**
- **Avoid damaging or changing wild animal habitats.**
- **Share your results with other scientists to reduce the number of animal experiments needed.**

Zoology labs have animal care technicians who look after the animals.

DO ZOOLOGISTS HAVE TO KILL ANIMALS?

Some animals, especially smaller ones such as insects, are still killed in order to study them, as long as they are not endangered and don't suffer. A sick animal might have to be put down, or you might work with animals like lizards, which have to be fed other animals, such as live grasshoppers.

However, you can mostly avoid this and still be a zoologist – for example by studying animal behavior instead of doing lab work.

IS ZOOLOGY YOUR OLOGY?

So you want to be a zoologist? Here's our handy guide on how to get there!

What makes a good zoologist?

To be a zoologist, these qualities and abilities will be a big help.

• Love animals!

You need to love animals and find them fascinating, as you're going to be spending a LOT of time with them.

• Sense of adventure

Zoology can take you to all kinds of amazing places around the world, so it's great if you like travel. Even if you work mainly in a lab, you'll do field work at some point. It often involves camping, hiking, and getting wet or muddy.

• Patience

You might have to sit around waiting for hours, days, or even weeks for an animal to do what you're interested in, or even just to show up!

• Organized and calm

You need to be able to keep careful records, operate sensitive equipment, and stay cool in a crisis.

SUBJECTS TO STUDY

When you choose subjects at school, which ones will help you become a zoologist?

Biology is the most useful – the science of living things.

Math, physics, chemistry, and computer science are good choices too.

Then you can study either biology or zoology in college.

How dangerous is zoology?

Zoology is classified as a high-risk job, as there are several dangers involved ...

- **Getting bitten, stung, or trampled**
- **Catching a disease from an animal**
- **Having an accident or getting lost while traveling in a remote area or out at sea.**

But you can reduce the risks by being careful and sensible!

What else could you do?

Besides being an actual zoologist, there are several other related jobs and activities ...

- Animal care technician in a zoology lab
- Zookeeper or zoo manager
- Vet or vet nurse
- Wildlife reserve warden, conservation volunteer, or campaigner
- Wildlife TV presenter, photographer, artist, or writer

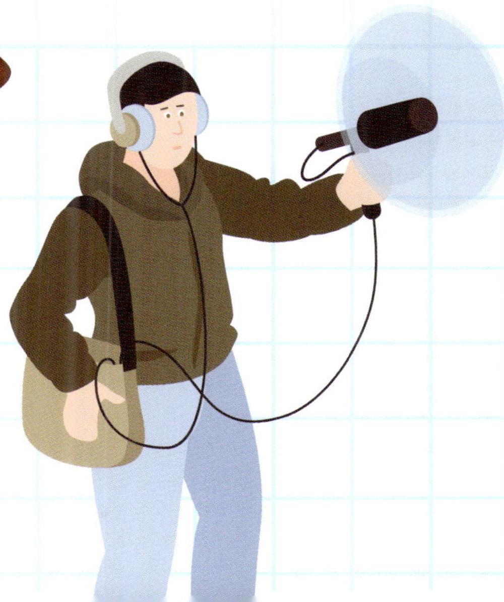

GLOSSARY

Adaptation Changing over time to suit the surroundings or conditions.

Algae A type of living thing that makes food using sunlight, similar to plants.

Amphibian A type of animal that spends part of its life in water, such as frogs and newts.

Anatomy The study of the shape and structure of the bodies of living things.

Arachnology The study of spiders and their relatives.

Arthropod A type of invertebrate animal with jointed legs, such as insects, spiders, and crabs.

Bacteria Very small, single-celled microorganisms, found in almost every habitat.

Biodiversity The variety of living things in a particular habitat, or in the whole world.

Biology The study of living things.

Bionics The science of using living things to inspire inventions and engineering.

Bird A type of vertebrate animal that has feathers and wings, and lays eggs.

Camera trap An automatic camera that is triggered to take a shot when it senses movement, used to monitor and count wild animals.

Carbon dioxide A type of gas found in the air, which contributes to global warming.

Cells The tiny units that living things are made up of.

Cetology The study of whales, dolphins, and porpoises.

Classification The process of sorting living things into types and groups.

Climate change A long-term change in climate patterns.

Computer simulation A simulation or copy of a real-life thing or situation programmed into a computer to help scientists study it.

Conservation Efforts to protect and preserve living species and natural habitats.

Coral reef A structure built on the seabed over a long time, by many generation of tiny sea creatures called coral polyps.

Courtship display A dance, show of color or other display, used by animals to attract a mate.

Crustacean A type of invertebrate animal that usually has a shell and many legs, such as crabs, shrimp, and woodlice.

DNA (short for deoxyribonucleic acid) A chemical found in cells, used to encode instructions that make the cell work.

Domestication The process of changing a species using selective breeding to make it more useful to humans.

Echinoderm A type of invertebrate animal with a body with five sections, such as starfish and sea urchins.

Ecology The study of ecosystems and how living things interact with one another.

Ecosystem A habitat and the community of living things that are found there.

Endangered At risk of dying out and becoming extinct.

Ethics Morals, or right and wrong ways of behaving.

Evolution A process of gradual change over multiple generations of living things.

Extinct To die out and no longer exist.

Felinology The study of cats.

Field "In the field" means in the wild, or in an animal's natural habitat.

Field station A building or camp used for studying animals in the field.

Fish A type of vertebrate water animal with a skeleton, fins, and gills.

Food web A network of plants and animals in an ecosystem that depend on each other for food.

Fungi A group of living things that includes mushrooms, molds, and yeast.

Genes Sequences of chemicals arranged along strands of DNA, which act as coded instructions for cells.

Genetic To do with genes.

Global warming A gradual increase in Earth's average temperature over the last two centuries, caused by human activities.

GPS (short for Global Positioning System) A system of satellites and receivers on the ground that can be used to show exactly where on the Earth's surface you are.

Habitat The natural home or surroundings of a living thing.

Herpetology The study of reptiles and amphibians.

Hydrophone A microphone that detects sound underwater.

Instinct A built-in, automatic pattern of behavior in an animal.

Invertebrate An animal without a backbone, such as an insect or a snail.

Krill A type of small sea crustacean.

Lab Short for laboratory, a room or building where scientists do tests or experiments.

Life cycle The series of changes a living thing goes through as it is born, grows, becomes an adult, and reproduces, or has young.

Mammal A type of living thing that feeds its babies milk made by their mother.

Marsupial A type of mammal that carries its babies in a pouch on the mother's underside.

Modeling Making a model of a real-life situation or thing to help you study it (see also **Computer simulation**).

Mollusk A soft-bodied type of invertebrate, such as snails and octopuses.

Monitoring Keeping track of a wild species and checking on its numbers, health, and movements.

Pollination Spreading pollen from one plant to another, which helps plants to make their seeds.

Predator An animal that hunts and eats other animals.

Prehistoric Dating from the time before people began to write down historic records.

Prey An animal that is hunted and eaten by another animal.

Reptile A type of living thing with scaly skin, such as lizards and snakes.

Scuba (short for Self-Contained Underwater Breathing Apparatus) diving Diving underwater with an oxygen supply carried on your back, so that you can breathe.

Selective breeding Changing living species over many generations by choosing individuals with useful qualities to breed from.

Species The scientific name for a particular type of living thing.

Tagging Attaching a special tag to an animal that sends out signals to help you track its movements.

Territory An area that an animal tries to control or thinks belongs to them.

Tracking Following the movements of a wild animal.

Vertebrate An animal with a backbone, such as a cat or a fish.

Wildlife reserve A wild area set aside for wildlife and protected to stop it from being changed or damaged by humans.

Further reading

BOOKS

Awesome Infographics: Endangered Animals
by Harriet Brundle and Heather Kissock
(AV2 Books, 2021)

Endangered Wildlife
by Anita Ganeri (Wayland, 2021)

The Who, What, Why of Zoology
By Jules Howard (Wide Eyed Editions, 2023)

WEBSITES

https://www.worldwildlife.org/
World Wide Fund for Nature conservation charity website.

www.iucnredlist.org
The IUCN Red List, where you can find out about all kinds of endangered species.

www.edgeofexistence.org
Edge of Existence, a conservation group helping a variety of endangered species.

www.fauna-flora.org
Flora and Fauna International, a global wildlife conservation organization.

Note to parents and teachers: every effort has been made by the Publishers to ensure websites are suitable for children, that they are of the highest educational value, and that they contain no inappropriate or offensive material. However, because of the nature of the Internet, it is impossible to guarantee that the contents of these sites will not be altered. We strongly advise that Internet access is supervised by a responsible adult.

INDEX